AFRICAN ANIMALS ABC

First U.S. Edition 1995

First published in the United Kingdom by Barefoot Books Ltd.

Library of Congress Cataloging-in-Publication data is available from Sierra Club Books for Children, 100 Bush Street, 13th Floor, San Francisco, California 94104.

Graphic design by Design/Section
Printed in Singapore
10 9 8 7 6 5 4 3 2

AFRICAN ANIMALS ABC

PHILIPPA-ALYS BROWNE

SIERRA CLUB BOOKS FOR CHILDREN

SAN FRANCISCO

Antbear naps

Bushbaby blinks

Crocodile snaps

Dassie drinks

Elephant lumbers

Frog leaps

Giraffe dozes

Hippo sleeps

Impala grazes

Jackal prowls

Kingfisher dives

Lion growls

Monkey chatters

Nyala shivers

Ostrich dances

Porcupine quivers

Quail scuttles

Rhino stomps

Secretary bird stretches

Tortoise chomps

Umhutu hums

Vulture mutters

Warthog charges

Xoona moth flutters

Yellow-billed kite soars in the sky

Zebra watches the world go by

ANIMAL NOTES

Here are some facts about each of the animals in the pictures. Some of the animal names are followed by "endangered" or "vulnerable," and, in some cases, "specially protected." "Endangered" means that the species of animal is in danger of extinction, or disappearing from the earth forever, and is unlikely to survive if the present factors for its decline continue. "Vulnerable" indicates a species that may become endangered if the reasons for its decline continue. "Specially protected" means that there are local or international laws to help prevent the vulnerable species from becoming endangered, or the endangered species from becoming extinct.

The size of each animal illustrated is given at the beginning of each description; the length includes the tail measurement, and the height is generally measured from the shoulder down.

ANTBEAR (*vulnerable*)

5 feet (1.5 m) long. The antbear, also called an aardvark, is a mammal found throughout Africa south of the Sahara. It lives alone and is active at night. During the day it sleeps in its underground burrow. The antbear digs into ant nests or termite mounds and licks out the ants or termites, which are its main food. Its tongue can reach nearly 12 inches (30 cm). The female gives birth to a single baby at a time.

BUSHBABY

14 to 28 inches (35 to 70 cm) long. There are several species of bushbaby, all found in Africa south of the Sahara. The thick-tailed bushbaby (shown in the picture) lives in eastern and southern Africa. Bushbabies are mammals that generally inhabit woodlands, where they eat fruit, seeds, leaves, insects, and small vertebrates (animals with backbones). They live alone, are active at night, and can leap great distances from tree to tree. At night bushbabies can be heard making loud child-like screams. The female gives birth to one or two young at a time.

CROCODILE (*vulnerable*)

15 feet (4 m) long or more. The crocodile is a reptile that lives in the warmer parts of Africa, Asia, Australia, and North and South America. The picture shows a Nile crocodile, which used to be found throughout Africa, but due to hunting it has disappeared from much of central and northern Africa. To maintain their body temperature crocodiles spend the day basking in the sun by rivers. They return to the water at midday, when it is too hot on the land, and in the evening, when the land cools down. They eat a variety of food, including weeds, insects, fish, large mammals, and even other crocodiles. Eggs are laid during the dry season and hatch four months later during the rainy season, when there is more food for the babies to eat.

DASSIE*

20 inches (50 cm) long. The dassie, or rock hyrax, is a mammal that, although only the size of a rabbit, is considered to be one of the nearest relatives of the elephant. The dassie is found throughout Africa in rock fields from plains to the tops of high mountains. Dassies live in groups and use their excellent eyesight and hearing to help them escape from danger. When threatened, a few individuals in the group will give warning barks or whistles. They feed for short periods in the morning and evening, and eat a mainly vegetarian diet, ranging from fruit to tree bark and twigs. The female gives birth to two or three offspring at a time.

Dassie means "rock hyrax" in Afrikaans (the language of South Africa).

ELEPHANT (*endangered**)

Up to 13 feet (4 m) tall. The elephant is a mammal and the largest living land animal. The African elephant (shown in the picture) is the biggest species of elephant. It is found throughout Africa south of the Sahara and lives in a variety of places, from grasslands to forests. Elephants live in family groups of "cows" (females) and their offspring or smaller groups of "bulls" (males). Old bulls often live alone. An adult elephant may eat up to 500 pounds (230 kg) of food a day because of its size. A typical elephant diet consists of grass, bark, pods, fruit, leaves, and other vegetation. The female gives birth year-round, producing one baby after a pregnancy of almost twenty-four months.

Its existence is not threatened in southern Africa, but it is regarded as endangered on the whole continent.

FROG

About 3 inches (8.5 cm) long. Tree frogs are found throughout Africa. Like all frogs, they are amphibians. They live mainly in trees, but a few live in water and some burrow in the ground. The foam nest tree frog (shown in the picture) inhabits trees in woodlands from the northeastern part of South Africa to Swaziland, Mozambique, Botswana, and Zimbabwe. It changes color from dark to light to blend in with its surroundings. It has clingy pads at the ends of its toes to help it climb, and it catches a variety of insects. The female lays up to 150 eggs during the rainy season in a foamy nest in a tree above water. When ready, the eggs hatch as tadpoles, bursting out of the foam and falling into the water below.

GIRAFFE

Up to 18 feet (5.5 m) tall from hoof to horn. Giraffes are found from southern Africa northward to Sudan and Ethiopia, and west to Senegal. They live in herds of from ten to as many as forty individuals, although the old "bulls" (males) often live alone. These tall mammals browse mainly on the shoots and twigs of acacia trees, but occasionally they can be seen grazing. Their senses of smell, sight, and hearing are excellent, and they can ward off predators with kicks or butts from the head. Calves are born throughout the year, one per female.

HIPPOPOTAMUS

Up to 4.5 feet (1.4 m) tall. The hippopotamus is a mammal distantly related to the pig. Unlike the pygmy hippopotamus, the common hippo (shown in the picture) is found throughout much of Africa south of the Sahara. Hippos live in or by large rivers or swampy areas with reed beds. Groups of up to twenty can be seen, although adult males often live alone. Hippos are active largely at night, when they graze on vast amounts of vegetation, often several miles away from water. During the day they sleep in the water, usually with their heads and backs above the surface. The female breeds at any time of the year and normally gives birth to one offspring at a time.

IMPALA

About 3 feet (90 cm) tall. The impala is a type of antelope that can be found browsing or grazing in brushy grasslands or open woodlands throughout southern Africa up to as far north as Kenya and Uganda, and west to Namibia and Angola. Impalas live in herds consisting of females and their young and a single dominant male. Bachelor herds of males live separately. When startled, impalas snort and dash off in high, bounding leaps that signal a warning to others. The female gives birth to one baby at a time.

JACKAL

Up to 16 inches (40 cm) tall. The jackal is a fox-like creature. The black-backed jackal (shown in the picture) is found in many areas of Africa, as well as in Asia and the Mideast, in light woodlands or on open plains. Jackals are active mostly at night and live alone or in pairs, although occasionally they live in family groups. Their diet ranges from fruit to rats, mice, reptiles, and birds. Jackal litters generally number six or more, and the young are born just after the rainy season.

KINGFISHER

18 inches (45 cm) long. Kingfishers are short-legged birds with dagger-like bills that live in many parts of the world. The giant kingfisher (shown in the picture) is found in all areas of Africa south of the Sahara, except the dry western parts. These alert birds live near wooded streams, lakes, and coastal lagoons, since their main food is fish. They live alone or, rarely, in pairs and are often seen perched on low branches or wire fences as they watch for activity in the water. The giant kingfisher breeds in holes in riverbanks or in trees. The female lays three to five eggs.

LION

Up to 3 feet (1 m) tall. Lions can be found from southern Africa north to the Sahara. These large cats inhabit all types of countryside except forest and live alone, in pairs, or in family groups, called "prides," of up to ten or more. They hunt both day and night, usually seeking large mammals as their prey. Lions breed throughout the year. The female leaves the pride to give birth, producing three or four cubs per litter.

MONKEY

Up to 4 feet (1.2 m) long. The vervet monkey (shown in the picture) is a mammal that can be found throughout much of Africa. These creatures live in open woodlands and bushy grasslands in troops numbering up to twenty. They eat mainly fruit, berries, leaves, roots, some insects, and occasionally other small animals. Most births are single; the baby often hangs from under the mother's belly or is carried in her arms.

NYALA

About 40 inches (1 m) tall. The nyala is a type of antelope that lives in southern Africa. It can be found grazing or browsing in grasslands, bush, and woodlands, usually near water. Nyalas live in small groups and are generally active from late afternoon through early morning. When startled, nyalas make barking sounds. The female gives birth to one baby at a time.

OSTRICH

Up to 6.5 feet (2 m) tall. This bird, which cannot fly, lives in isolated pockets throughout southern Africa, in areas ranging from woodlands to grasslands, bush, and desert regions. It eats grass, succulent plants, berries, insects, and small reptiles, and swallows stones to help with its digestion. The ostrich can run extremely fast—up to 40 miles (60 km) per hour. When the male is excited, it often fills its throat with air to make a lion-like roar. Each male mates with several females, who each lay three to eight eggs in the same shallow hole. Both the male and female take turns tending the eggs, which take five to eight weeks to hatch.

PORCUPINE

2.5 feet (80 cm) long. The southern African crested porcupine (shown in the picture) is found in any type of countryside throughout much of Africa south of the Sahara. This rodent lives alone, in pairs, or in family groups, and is active mainly at night. It makes a grunting, snuffling noise like a pig. The porcupine spends its day in a cave or hole that it or another type of animal has dug. Its diet is vegetarian. When threatened, it raises its quills, which are up to 1 foot (40 cm) long, and charges backward toward its attacker. The female gives birth to one to three young at a time.

QUAIL

7 inches (18 cm) long. There are about 130 species of quail throughout the world. The harlequin quail (shown in the picture) lives in pairs and is found primarily on grasslands,

pastures, and cultivated fields throughout Africa. These birds spend most of their time on the ground and eat mainly seeds, shoots, and insects. When disturbed, they may make piercing alarm cries. The female lays up to twelve eggs at a time.

RHINOCEROS (*endangered/specially protected*)

Up to 6.5 feet (1.6 m) tall. White (shown in the picture) and black rhinos, which once lived throughout Africa, are now found only in highly protected pockets south of the Sahara. The white rhinoceros generally grazes during the cooler times of the day and lives alone, in pairs, or in family groups. It is found only on grassy plains, while the black rhino favors dense and thorny bush. Rhinos have poor eyesight but a keen sense of smell, and they communicate with one another by making grunting, snorting, and squealing sounds. A female gives birth to one baby every three to four years.

SECRETARY BIRD (*vulnerable/specially protected*)

4 feet (1.25 m) tall. These large birds generally live in pairs and can be seen walking through grasslands and bush in areas of Africa south of the Sahara. When flying, they may soar at a great height and, on landing, run a short distance with outspread wings. Secretary birds eat insects, snakes, tortoises, young birds, and any small animal they can kill. They attack snakes using violent blows from their feet. They roost near the tops of small trees, and when disturbed they make frog-like croaks. Breeding occurs throughout the year, with each female laying two or three eggs at a time.

TORTOISE

Up to 1 foot (30 cm) tall. (A hinged tortoise is shown in the picture.) This hard-shelled reptile lives in a variety of regions, from dry countryside to riverside forest. It is found in central and eastern South Africa, as well as Mozambique, Zimbabwe, and northern Botswana. During the day the hinged tortoise eats small insects and vegetation. In the evening it rests in a shallow hole that it digs in a protected place, such as a rocky bank or a termite mound. Its shell provides armor-like protection as well as good camouflage. The female lays one to five eggs a year.

UMHUTU*

About .10 inch (3 mm) long. The umhutu, or mosquito, is an insect. Various species of this insect can carry diseases such as malaria and yellow fever. The common household mosquito (shown in the picture) is found throughout Africa. It will breed in almost any pool of stagnant water, laying a large number of eggs. These hatch into larvae, which become adult mosquitoes in about two to three weeks. Only the female mosquito sucks blood; the male lives on flower nectar and the juices of ripe fruit.

*Umhutu means "mosquito" in Shona (the language of the Mashona tribe of Zimbabwe).

VULTURE (*vulnerable/specially protected*)

About 3 feet (1 m) tall. Vultures are scavengers and are found on many continents besides Africa. The lappet-faced vulture (shown in the picture) occurs throughout most of Africa, except the most heavily forested areas. These birds live in pairs in the bush or desert. They feed on the flesh of dead animals and spend much of their day soaring in the sky searching for food. Normally they make no noise, but when squabbling over food they hiss and squeal. The female generally lays only one egg in a nest made of sticks in a tree or on a rocky ledge.

WARTHOG

Up to 2.5 feet (75 cm) tall. This pig-like creature is widespread in Africa, usually living on grasslands where there are some trees and bushes to give cover. Warthogs live alone or in family groups. During the heat of the day they often sleep; in the cool of the evening they forage for roots and fruit. When disturbed, the warthog dashes through the bush with its tail held erect like an aerial. The female gives birth to as many as six offspring at a time.

XOONA* MOTH

Wingspan up to 2.5 inches (6 cm). A moth is a flying insect that is active mainly at night. The cream-striped owl moth (shown in the picture) is common throughout Africa south of the Sahara. It is attracted to rotting fruit and to sweet and alcoholic drinks. This moth lays thousands of eggs, which hatch into caterpillars that feed on acacia trees.

*Xoona means "owl" in Tsonga (the language of the Tsonga tribe of Mozambique).

YELLOW-BILLED KITE

22 inches (55 cm) long. Kites are large, long-winged birds of prey with v-shaped tails. The yellow-billed kite (shown in the picture) is found throughout Africa. It spends most of the day soaring low, looking for prey — generally small animals such as mice, rats, snakes, and other birds. It also scavenges large animals. The kite's nest consists of a platform of sticks laid in a tree; often it is lined with dung, wool, and hide. The female lays two or three eggs at a time.

ZEBRA

Just over 4 feet (1.3 m) tall. All species of this horse-like animal live in Africa. The Burchell's zebra (shown in the picture) is found from South Africa to Sudan, Ethiopia, and Somalia. Zebras generally live on tree- and bush-dotted grasslands where they roam in large herds, often with wildebeests, roans, impalas, and even ostriches. They neigh like horses but make high-pitched barks or squeals when fighting or alarmed. Zebras produce offspring throughout the year, with a peak during the rainy season. The female gives birth to one foal at a time.